OUR ACTIONS
Will Show

PASTOR WILBERT WATSON

Copyright © 2024 Pastor Wilbert Watson.

All rights reserved. No part of this book may be reproduced, stored, or transmitted by any means—whether auditory, graphic, mechanical, or electronic—without written permission of both publisher and author, except in the case of brief excerpts used in critical articles and reviews. Unauthorized reproduction of any part of this work is illegal and is punishable by law.

ISBN: 979-8-89419-277-2 (sc)
ISBN: 979-8-89419-278-9 (hc)
ISBN: 979-8-89419-279-6 (e)

Because of the dynamic nature of the Internet, any web addresses or links contained in this book may have changed since publication and may no longer be valid. The views expressed in this work are solely those of the author and do not necessarily reflect the views of the publisher, and the publisher hereby disclaims any responsibility for them.

One Galleria Blvd., Suite 1900, Metairie, LA 70001
(504) 702-6708

CONTENTS

Preface v

Dedication vii

Chapter 1   It's Not Enough to Just Talk 1

Chapter 2   Being on Fire Serving the Lord 8

Chapter 3   People With Genuine Faith Will Remain 14

Chapter 4   Refuse to Give Up 20

Chapter 5   Listen for The Holy Spirit's Guidance.............. 28

Chapter 6   Know The Spirit of Truth and Error................. 37

Chapter 7   Show Your Best Character and Conduct 44

Chapter 8   Gotta Keep Moving Forward 51

Chapter 9   Know God's Will For Your Life 57

Chapter 10 Being Busy is No Excuse................................... 62

Chapter 11 We Must Be Doers of the Word........................ 66

Chapter 12 Always Be Ready, to Give a Defense!................74

PREFACE

In Luke 6:45 (ESV) Jesus says, *"The good person out of the good treasure of his heart produces good, and the evil person out of his evil treasure produces evil, for out of the abundance of the heart his mouth speaks."*

What's truly in our heart, will flow out of our mouth; whether that be good or bad. If we proclaim that we believe, love and following Jesus Christ as our Lord and Savior; our actions can contradict what we're really saying and believe. Many are saying and thinking they believe in Jesus Christ but their actions show otherwise. Our actions reveal the truth about who we really love: ourselves or God. If our words and actions are saying different things we must examine our actions for the truth. The purpose of this book is to help many know for certain; if they are genuine followers and believers in Jesus Christ.

DEDICATION

*This book is dedicated to my mom. The woman who gave me life and helped shape me into the person I am today.
Thank you for praying faithfully all those years.
Your prayers made all the difference.
Thank you for always loving me and guiding me. Even though you are no longer here with me, I can still feel your love guiding me. You are always in my heart.
I love you, honor you, and miss you dearly.
This book is for you, Mom! Long live the memories and your love for God, your children, and many others.*

Ms. Flora B. Dixon
July 30, 1939 – November 23, 2023

Thank you for purchasing

Our Actions Will Show!

This book highlights our words and actions are a manifestation of our true character. It is an indication of a what's truly in our hearts.

Chapter 1

IT'S NOT ENOUGH TO JUST TALK

1 John 3:18-19 (KJV), states, *"¹⁸My little children, let us not love in word, neither in tongue; but indeed, and in truth. ¹⁹And hereby we know that we are of the truth, and shall assure our hearts before him"*.

We've all probably heard the saying or adage; *"actions speak louder than words, and true credibility comes from what one does, not just what one says."*

It's not enough to just talk! God's Word is challenging us to live-up to what we say. Are we walking-the-walk, or just talking- the talk? Our actions will really show if we are walking the walk, or just talking the talk.

I believe it was James Brown, the god father of soul, would say: "Talkin' Loud and Sayin' Nothing." What we say, especially, concerning to God; we must also demonstrate through our actions. Lip service is totally insufficient without actions, and a humble heart. Mere lip service is being a hypocrite in God's eyes.

Sincere people really committed to God; actions will not be different from their words. They will walk-the-walk, and talk-the-talk; they will not worship God by words of mouth alone but demonstrate it by their actions. Glory to God!

In 1 John chapter 3, the Apostle John summarizes the need for Christians to act on love, not just think about it. It is important to communicate love through our words, but we must also do so through our actions.

I love keeping it real; it's not enough just to just "talk the talk." The true believers must also "walk the walk. Many people are willing to talk about their faith and about the Lord. Sadly, many actions and conduct, are not in-line with God's words, or His command. They are talking the talk, but not walking the walk. In other words; they are just "hearers only" of God's Word, they are not the faithful doers of God's Word.

This is not pleasing to God, and He deals with this issue significantly, according to His Word. I pray that chapter one of this book help many to do a real heartfelt or deep self-examination that leads to faithfully "walking the talk. We as believers must show through our actions that we are walking the walk, and talking the talk. Mean what you say, you are going to do.

Both in John's Day and today; we find those who say: "I know the Lord. But they "do not do" what the Lord commands." The apostle John says, that such professing believers, who do not do what Jesus commands, are liars. That said, there are three ways to graciously deal with liars and deceivers, even in the church:

1) Pray for them
2) Confront the liar with truth
3) Ignore their lies and accusations

I will now expound on the three ways mentioned above:

1) **Pray for them** - We should keep on praying for them (the liars); God knows how to deal with liars and deceivers.

As a matter of fact, God can deal with them before we even try to talk to them to address an issue.

2) ***Confront the liar with truth*** - We can lovingly confront or handle the lie with the truth. Lies can only be dispelled or ousted with the truth.

When we confront the liar with the truth, he/she can then be given the opportunity to admit the lie, and repent of it. Follow the Matthew 18:15-17 way of dealing with a sinning brother in the church: personally talk to him/her alone:

- If he doesn't listen, bring a witness;
- If he still doesn't listen, bring the matter to the church;
- If he still doesn't listen, just let him be a stranger to you.

Please keep in mind that the motivation for this is to bring a sinning brother to the Lord through repentance, so that he/she may be restored.

3) ***Ignore their lies and accusations*** - Lastly, by the enabling grace and confidence that God gives, we should ignore the lies.

I am not advocating we should just allow anybody to slander or insult us. What I am saying is we should not let the lies and accusations distress or shake us. If there's nothing to hide, there's nothing to fear anyway. If we have a clear conscience before the Lord, then we're good. Let us not take revenge against the liar, rather, let us do what pleases the Lord. He is our vindicator (see Romans 12:19; Psalm 4:1-4).

> 1 John 2:4, says, *"Whoever says, "I know him," but does not do what he commands is a liar, and the truth is not in that person."*

Yes, I realize these are very strong words, but they are God's Word, not mines. Honoring God with just our lips is vain worship! According to Matthew 15:9, *vain worship is worship that is based on man-made doctrine (rule) and a wrong view of God. Basically, vain worship is man-centered and self-serving; it's not God centered.*

Vain worship also includes embracing God as loving, kind and merciful without accepting that He is also just, righteous, holy, wrathful and vengeful. Isaiah 29:13, states, *"these people draw near to me with their mouths, and honors me with their lips, yet have removed their hearts far from me. Moreover, their worship toward me is the doctrines of men."*

These people; while the Israelites were saying the right things, their hearts were far from God! Sounds familiar? When God said that "their hearts are far from me," He meant that the Israelites had chosen other loyalties besides God. While they might have sounded religious; they did not love God or obey Him. Their thoughts and their decisions were bent or turned away from God.

As for an example: Even by the time the Messiah, Jesus Christ had come, many religious leaders were false in their worship. God was honored in words, but insulted in practice.

The problem with so much of our worship today is most of it does not involve or engaged with sacrifice. True worship has an outcome that is good for everyone. Worship is more than just singing songs. If we worship God in a way that is truly sacrificial, we will impact the people around us, and they will "give honor" to God; they will worship God. But if we worship God in the way many are doing these days; most people will stay unmoved or disinterested, and detached or disconnected from church.

I said previously, as an example: Even by the time the Messiah had come, many religious leaders were false in their worship. God was honored in words, but insulted in practice.

Another example is when Jesus cleansed the temple by driving-out those who were violating or desecrating it. Jesus said, *"It is written, My house shall be called a house of prayer but you have made it a den of robbers"* (Matthew 21:12-13, Isaiah 56:7).

Jesus drives-out the money changers and merchants, and he overturns or turn-over the money-changers' tables. Jesus, also heals some blind and lame people and refuses to silence some children who are praising Him, as the Son of David. The title "Son of David" is more than a statement of physical genealogy. It is a Messianic title!

When people referred to Jesus as the Son of David, they meant that He was the long-awaited Deliverer; the fulfillment of the Old Testament prophecies. Jesus was addressed as "Lord, thou son of David" several times by people who, by faith, were seeking mercy or healing. First John 3:18-19 (KJV), says, *"My little children, let us not love in word, neither in tongue; but indeed, and in truth."*

We as believers (God's children) cannot minister to people as we should, if we are not walking in love, and in the light. We must strive to have a heart that is right before God and men (Acts 24:16). Ask God to use you to be an encouragement and help to others. Love is more than a matter of words.

Jesus gave a similar warning to the Pharisees in Matthew 15:4–9 (NIV):

> [4]For God said, 'Honor your father and mother' and 'Anyone who curses their father or mother is to be put to death.'
>
> [5]But you say that if anyone declares that what might have been used to help their father or mother is 'devoted to God,'
>
> [6]they are not to 'honor their father or mother' with it. Thus, you nullify the word of God for the sake of your tradition.
>
> [7]You hypocrites! Isaiah was right when he prophesied about you:
>
> [8]"'These people honor me with their lips, but their hearts are far from me. [9]They worship me in vain; their teachings are merely human rules.'"

While the Pharisees criticize Jesus for not following a man-made rule, they themselves use man-made rules to avoid following the actual commands of God! The Pharisees still did religious things but had forgotten the reasons behind their actions. They said the right things, but their hearts were far from God. One might faithfully go to church every Sunday but ignore God, the rest of the week. Like the Pharisees and the ancient Israelites, "faking it" is not spiritually healthy, and it will eventually catch up with you.

Everyone who does evil hates the Light, and does not come into the Light for fear that his deeds will be exposed (John 3:20). One cannot walk with God and with Demons at the Same Time. God's word (the Bible) says, "if your heart is not right before God, you have no part or portion in this matter. Being just before God is what gives us peace before Him. God requires devotion, dedication, and the constant presentation of our bodies, souls, and spirits to His service.

In conclusion of chapter one; if we are half-hearted, self-satisfied, and indifferent to God's glory, our hearts are not right in the sight of God. Even if our hearts condemn us, God is greater than our hearts, and He knows all things. God does not give lip service, and He does everything He says He will do. If we claim to worship God, and it's not from our hearts, know that Jesus will rebuke us. Honoring God with only our lips, while our actions show a different story will cause us to get rebuked by the Lord. Truly loving another person will produce loving actions; it's not enough to just talk. We are to walk the walk and talk the talk.

NOTES:

Chapter 2

BEING ON FIRE SERVING THE LORD

Romans 12:11-12 (NIV), says, *"¹¹Never be lacking in zeal, but keep your spiritual fervor, serving the Lord. ¹²Be joyful in hope, patient in affliction, faithful in prayer."*

Even though it's not enough to just talk about serving the Lord; God is faithful and keeps His promises even when we are faithless. This chapter is to encourage Christians to be on fire serving the Lord. Our personal attitude matters when serving, the Lord. One attitude that keeps us from serving God wholeheartedly; is laziness. Laziness makes our hearts lukewarm and comfortable. Laziness has no place in the character or personality of a follower of Jesus because our personal attitude matters when serving the Lord. In affliction or sickness, distress, trouble, or pressure; we as believers, are to be patient. We are to be steadfast (unwavering) with endurance or Perseverance. Plus, we should continue in prayer to God for wisdom, guidance, and strength. Be faithful to God!

Being on fire serving the Lord" involves expressing love and adoration for Him, recognizing the Lord's worthiness, and responding with real or true worship both in private and public settings. We must have a burning desire for God that leads to a life of obedience to His commandments. Being on fire for God involves utilizing our talents or spiritual gifts to build-up the body of Christ.

I want to encourage you and many others to stay on fire for the Lord. First Corinthians 13 makes it very clear; unless our service is rooted in love, it's meaningless. I don't want my love or serving the Lord to be worthless or useless. Serving God out of a sense of obligation or duty, apart from love for God, is not what God desires. Instead, serving God should be our natural, love-filled response to Him who loved us first (1 John 4:9–11). Our mindset or attitude should be; we are serving the Lord; therefore, don't be lazy, work hard! God has given us spiritual gifts to be used in serving Him (Romans 12:3-8). When we use those spiritual gifts to serve God's kingdom purposes; He energizes us with His power.

It's important to understand that laziness leads to unfruitfulness, in God's Kingdom. One of the shocking or devastating biblical consequences of laziness is; it leads to poverty or lack. This explains why some people are poor or lack as they are not willing to work with their God-given hands. We as believers may be free to "retire" from our job or career, but as disciples or followers of Jesus Christ, we are not ever free to retire from serving God and others. We are to stay accountable and remain or stay on fire for God.

Genuine or real service cannot be separated from love. Yes, people can go through the gestures or the motions of serving God but if their hearts are not in it; they are really missing the point. Remember Romans 12:11 (NIV)?

> *"Never be lacking in zeal, but keep your spiritual fervor, serving the Lord."*

We are part of the Body of Jesus Christ with a ministry to fulfill. We are to Do our part; lovingly and joyfully. This way, we can keep our spiritual passion boiling or hot in the Holy Spirit. We are called to be on fire with the Holy Spirit and to serve the Lord actively and zealously. Never be lacking in zeal serving the Lord. Be joyful in hope, patient in affliction and faithful in prayer. God expect us to be faithful in prayer. To be faithful in prayer requires that we understand prayer is expected, effective and must not be ousted or exhausted. Faithfulness in prayer means praying regularly and often. Our prayers should be saturated or flooded with praise and thanksgiving to God, our heavenly Father. Rejoice in our confident hope, be patient in trouble, and keep on praying.

> Ephesians 6:18, says, *"And pray in the Spirit on all occasions with all kinds of prayers and requests. With this in mind, be alert and always keep on praying for all the Lord's people."*

Praying "in the Spirit" means to pray with the mind of the Spirit. When we pray "in the Spirit," we are praying according to the will of God. Praying according to the will of God not only assures us that He hears our prayers. God will answer our prayers in His own way and in His own time.

Genuine Christians should not offer their service to God half-heartedly or in a lazy manner. We are to serve God eagerly and in earnest. Many don't realize that half-heartedness in serving God, is a serious mistake. Half-heartedness or laziness gives no satisfaction to our Lord. Half-heartedly serving the Lord will lead one to darkness, doubt, worldliness, and guilt.

Being on fire for God involves utilizing our talents or spiritual gifts to build-up the body of Christ. Our primary focus should be on what God desires for us and not on what the world wants us to do. Being "on fire for God" means having a passionate love for and dedication to God, and it is important to not let worldly influences hinder our love, passion and dedicated service to God.

Keeping it very real! Being on fire for God means not being afraid to take a stand, and make a difference in the world, despite the opposition. It is being wanted or required to go the extra mile and to do whatever it takes to bring glory to God. Glory hallelujah!

> First Corinthians 15:58, reads, *Therefore, my dear brothers and sisters, stand firm. Let nothing move you. Always give yourselves fully to the work of the Lord, because you know that your labor in the Lord is not in vain.*

As real Christians, our primary focus should be on what God desires for us and not on what the world wants us to do. Pleasing God is, or should be, the goal of all real believers. We do this by being obedient to God and by the power of His Holy Spirit who lives in our hearts. Glory to God!

It's time to Go back, to your first love! Revelation 2:4, speaks of the first love that has been abandoned so many times. Our first love is and will always be Jesus. What keeps us focused on Christ as our first love is this great reminder that it was, He who loved us first and our love for Him now comes simply as a response to the greatest love we will ever know.

In conclusion of chapter 2; "Being on fire for God" is to have a passionate and intense love, and devotion for Him to the point where it motivates and inspires one's actions and decisions. Being on fire for God often involves a strong desire to "live a life that glorifies God" and to share one's faith with others. It involves having a passionate devotion to God's presence that springs from a heart-filled with the Lord Himself. In our hearts, the fire of God is burning. When we pray in the Holy Spirit; the fire is fanned and grows brighter, ultimately consuming everything that is not of God.

"Let your light so shine before men, that they may see your good works and glorify your Father in heaven." (Matthew 5:16) The desire to serve and be devoted to God comes from deep within your heart. It is a fire that can never be extinguished, no matter the circumstances or how much time passes. It is a feeling that grows and strengthens each day, slowly but surely consuming you until it is all-inclusive or all-encompassing. The longing to be closer to God is a powerful emotion. It moves you to action and helps to guide your decisions. This burning passion can be so strong that it sometimes becomes a burden, as you search for ways to put your faith into practice.

The love for God is a sacred flame that can never be put out.

GLORY TO GOD!

It is a flame that warms your soul and fills you with light. It is a comfort in times of darkness and a joy in moments of happiness. Even when the fire is low, it never completely leaves you. God is always there, and so is your desire to serve Him. Be on fire, serving The Lord!

NOTES:

Chapter 3

PEOPLE WITH GENUINE FAITH WILL REMAIN

Our actions are true indicators of what's actually in our hearts. It's clearly noticeable that one's faith is not true faith when they are merely talking about their faith love for Jesus Christ.

> John 15:5 (NIV), says, *"I am the vine; you are the branches. If you remain in me and I in you, you will bear much fruit; apart from me you can do nothing."*

People with genuine faith will remain; they abide in Christ Jesus, stay close to Him, and follow His lead. Abiding in Christ Jesus equips us to bear the fruit of the Spirit, the foundation of the faithful life. It's important to live a faithful life and submit our lives to the will of God. People of God, remain faithful. When we are certain or convinced that God's Words, are true and faithful.

Living a faithful life becomes a new nature within us that produces or gives us a desire to live in a way that pleases God. I pray that this chapter encourages people to Live faithful lives, and remain faithful; no matter what. John 15:5 describes the real meaning of a fruitful Christian life. Jesus compares the abundant life He offers to a relationship between a vine and its branches. Without Jesus Christ; we can do nothing. John 15:5, refers to the interruption of fellowship and dependency upon the Lord.

By faith, we must stay connected to Jesus Christ every second of every day to live the most God-honoring and abundant life of peace and fruitfulness in Christ Jesus. Because we can do nothing apart from Christ. A believer cannot accomplish anything of permanent spiritual value without Jesus Christ. Jesus says, *I am the vine; you are the branches. If you remain in me and I in you, you will bear much fruit; apart from me "you can do nothing."*

Not abiding in Christ Jesus has serious consequences. To "abide" is to live, continue, or remain; to abide in Christ is to live in Him or remain in Him. When a person is saved, he or she is described as being "in Christ" (Romans 8:1; 2 Corinthians 5:17), held secure in a permanent relationship (John 10:28–29). Therefore, abiding in Christ is not a special level of Christian experience, rather, it is the position of all true believers.

The difference between those abiding in Christ and those not abiding in Christ is the difference between the saved and the unsaved. Yes, the saved or unsaved. I will expound on this; those not abiding in Christ is the difference between the saved and the unsaved. According to God's word (the Bible), a person is saved when he accepts that he is a sinner, repents for his sins, and by faith, accepts the free gift of salvation made possible by Jesus' sacrifice on the cross.

Salvation is a gift of God; not a result of works. The Bible says, that "if you confess with your mouth the Lord Jesus, and believe in your heart that God raised him from the dead, you will be saved." A person is either forever saved or was never saved. The Bible teaches that once you are a believer in Christ, your salvation is forever secure in him. However, once you are a believer in Christ Jesus, you can later reject his salvation. The gift of salvation is not a gift to be taken lightly, and it means that we are bound to do what Jesus would do; veering or deviating away from sin, because the life of a Christian is a never-ending journey to be faithful to Christ.

Jesus defined "Abiding in Christ" when He compared Himself to the true vine and believers to its branches:

> "Abide in Me, and I in you. John 15:4, reads *"As the branch cannot bear fruit of itself, unless it abides in the vine, so, neither can you, unless you abide in Me."*

The picture shows that to us, the essential union that exist between Christians and Jesus Christ. The word "abide" essentially means "to remain." Every Christian remains devoted or connected to Christ in all areas of life. We depend on Christ for grace and power to obey. We look obediently to His Word for instruction on how to live. We offer the Lord our deepest adoration and praise, and we submit ourselves to His authority over our lives. Genuine believers in Christ Jesus gratefully know that He is the source and sustainer of their lives. Without Jesus, we can do nothing! Jesus says without me; you can do nothing; our greatest need is to stay deeply connected with Christ (John 15:4-10).

Notice how John 15:4, repeatedly mentions that God wants us to abide in Him, and if we do that He will abide (remain) in us. But why abide or remain in us? Because God loves us; he wants us transformed into the likeness of Jesus Christ. God wants to love on us, because our spiritual growth, is important to Him. We cannot accomplish anything of permanent, spiritual value because spiritual values help us to love God and completely submit to God, such as reverence and compassion. A human being develops spiritual values throughout his or her life.

I need to make something very clear about loss of fellowship with God. As genuine (true) believers in Christ Jesus; when we sin, we do not lose our fellowship with God. Fellowship is our intimacy or closeness with God. It's impossible because Jesus has finished everything required by the Father to get us into fellowship with Him and to keep us there. It's totally based on Jesus' victorious work on the cross; not our behavior. There is no Scripture that says a Christian breaks fellowship with God when he or she sins. If that were the case, every Christians would constantly be breaking fellowship with God.

Romans 14:23 defines sin as "not living by faith," that is, not living dependent on God. If we are not depending on God, we are depending on our flesh. The context of Romans 14:23 is certainly in the context of eating meat sacrificed to idols, but it is a truth which transcends that issue. Any time a person lives even one second depending on their flesh, rather than God, He considers it sin. This means we all may sin a lot more often than we are aware.

The word "fellowship" means partnership or partaker. So, with this in mind, fellowship with God is two-fold. The first has to do with our wonderful position of our union with God the moment of our salvation.

> First Corinthians 6:17 says, *"But the one who joins himself to the Lord is (1) One Spirit with Him, and (2) that union cannot be broken by a Christian's sin."*

As believers obey Christ's word and abide in his love; they come to experience and understand his love for them more and more. Jesus Christ desires us to know, commune and fellowship with Him on a moment-by-moment basis. Abiding in Christ Jesus proves genuine salvation. The Apostle John mentioned that when he referred to defected professors in (1 John 2:19; NIV):

> *"They went out from us, but they did not really belong to us. For if they had belonged to us, they would have remained with us; but their going showed that none of them belonged to us."*

People with genuine faith will remain; they won't defect or change sides. They won't deny Christ or abandon His truth. Jesus reiterated the importance of abiding as a sign of real faith when He said, in John 8:31: *"If you abide in My Word, then you are truly disciples of Mine."*

Please take a just a brief moment to call, text or email two or three people, and tell them "Stay connected" to Jesus Christ!

It's best to interpret or understand the True Vine metaphor, this way: obviously, Jesus is the True Vine. The branches who "abide" in Him are the truly saved; they have a real and vital connection to the Savior. The withered branches who do not "abide" in Jesus Christ are the unsaved pretenders who put-on or faked an attachment to the Vine but drew no life from Him (the Lord).

In conclusion, in the end, pretenders will be seen for what they were; followers who had no authentic or true attachment or connection to Jesus. If you recall; for a while, both Peter and Judas seemed the same or alike in their walk with Christ. But Peter was connected to the Vine, Judas was not. One of the proofs of salvation is perseverance, or sustained abiding in Christ Jesus.

The saved will continue in their walk with Christ (see Revelation 2:26). Those who fall away, turn their backs on Christ, or fail to abide simply show their lack of saving faith. Abiding is not what saves us, but it is one of the signs of salvation. People with genuine faith, will remain or stay connected to the body of Christ Jesus. People with genuine faith will remain or stay connected to the body of Christ, no matter what! Are You, one of the people with genuine faith? Our greatest need as believers is to stay deeply connected with Christ (John 15:4-10). Genuine faith is sincere and real! Genuine faith is solid, unchanging, and remains for a lifetime. It's not fake, nor is it temporary (2 Timothy 1:5). People with genuine faith will remain!

NOTES:

Chapter 4

REFUSE TO GIVE UP

We as cannot pull back or withdraw the decisions, we've already made in life. We can only affect the decisions we're going to make, from here on out. Successful believers in Christ Jesus, keep it moving; yes, they make mistakes, but they don't quit! because they Refuse, To Give Up! People will always find someone to talk about; but they don't know your journey, where you've been or where you're going. Give your attention to the opinions that matter or ignore them all if you like. The only one who can make you give up, is yourself. When somebody tells you; you can't do something; oftentimes, they are only telling you what they cannot do.

> Galatians 6:9-10 (NIV), says, *"9 Let us not become weary in doing good, for at the proper time we will reap a harvest if we do not give up. 10 Therefore, as we have opportunity, let us do good to all people, especially to those who belong to the family of believers."*

Refuse, to give up; refuse to give up on doing good! In the Bible, God recognizes the reality of weariness. Because weariness can cause us to forget that God is along for the journey; he is with us on our daily walk. Weariness is a condition of the heart and spirit. There is an unhealthy or damaging type of weariness that strives in the power of the flesh. It's the result of foolish or misguided motives. Perhaps, we become driven by the fear of people. We are worried or preoccupied with not wanting to let someone down. If, our fear of people transcends or exceeds our fear of God; we default into performance-based living. It saps or drains our energy, and leaves us feeling depleted or exhausted. Worry is wearisome, and fear, is fatiguing.

> Romans 8:6, says, *"The mind governed by the flesh is death, but the mind governed by the Spirit, is life and peace."*

The Lord is your hope and strength, but even as you experience accomplishments, you can quickly lose faith because you have not cultivated a hopeful heart. Sometimes we are so sick and tired, or weary of dealing with drama, a family member or a child or children with a horrible or foul mouth; an attitude that we are weary.

Sometimes we are so frustrated or exasperated, and disappointed from dealing with someone from church, or our extended family, work, or at another activity or action – that we are weary. No matter the weary situation or circumstance; we may find ourselves in refuse to give up.

Just like the Sower of seed (Jesus Christ) must wait for the harvest; the Christian must wait patiently for the rewards that will inevitably come from the Giver of all good things (James 1:17). We will not give up because our Lord is faithful! Always give yourselves fully to the work of the Lord because you know that your labor in the Lord is not in vain (1 Corinthians 15:58).

Those who genuinely "do good" will be tempted soon enough to grow weary. Weariness can be contagious (Deuteronomy 20:8) but when we fight back; it also can work the other way, to help others persevere. God means for us not only to endure in "doing good" ourselves, but to help others "not grow weary" (1 Thessalonians 5:14). Don't lose heart in doing good, for in due time we will reap if we do not grow weary.

God did not rescue us from sin and death, to do nothing; He wants his people to give their lives, to what precious little time they have, to "doing good." Galatians 6:10, says, *"As we have opportunity, let us do good to everyone, and especially to those who are of the household of faith."*

Doing good is not just for peaceful, convenient times in our lives, but just as much for seasons of suffering and conflict. "Let those who suffer according to God's will entrust their souls to a faithful Creator while doing good" (1 Peter 4:19). When Christ gives us a particular calling to fulfill, he definitely does not promise that it will come easy. In fact, it is often precisely, the opposite. Difficult obstacles appear or emerge to confirm the genuineness of our calling. The breakthrough will come not in retreat but in enduring under trial with faith in God's promises.

We may even swell in hope as obstacles increase, anticipating the BREAKTHROUGH, we need may be near at hand. As Believers, in Christ Jesus, we do not need to grow weary in doing good because God makes a promise to all believers that if they stay strong and continue to do good, believers will reap a harvest at the proper time (Galatians 6:9).

God's never early, never late, but always on time; our timing is not God's timing. For us, God's timing often feels like a long desperate delay. But God's perfect timing does two things:

    (1) It grows our faith as we are forced to wait and trust in God; and

    (2) it makes certain that God, and He alone, gets the glory and praise, for pulling us through.

The apostle Paul has just asked the Galatian Christians to be convinced once again that trusting their flesh in this life will only lead to corruption. Reliance on our own power only leads to decay and death. We cannot allow ourselves to get tired of living the right way. We can't allow ourselves to get tired of living the right way. Certainly, each of us will receive everlasting life at the proper time, if we don't give up!

When life pushes you over, it's easy to give up and let the situation ruin your entire life. But when you refuse to give up; you stay focused on your goals and are not afraid to tackle the toughest or hardest challenges. Strong willpower is a powerful tool, you need to overcome tough times. You cannot live a successful life with a weak will power. Oftentimes, people are tempted to quit believing because they get tired or worn-out. I am sure, many of us have felt that very same temptation.

God promises us: "Let us not become weary in doing good, for at the proper time we will reap a harvest if we do not give up." We are encouraged to remain steadfast (committed), our time of waiting will eventually, produce a harvest. The manifestation of what we've been waiting for and believing to see will happen.

> "It is impossible to live without failing at something, unless you live so cautiously that you might as well not have lived at all, in which case you have failed by default." — J.K. Rowling

What Most people don't realize is, failure acts as a stepping-stone towards success. It's through our greatest failures, we learn more about life, love, goals, happiness, and all the things that make us into who we are today. Never give up on something you really want; it's difficult to wait but it's more difficult to regret. All the trials you go through in life, are making you stronger. You will go through trials and get out, and then sometimes, go back in them but always remember, the mighty hand of God, is at work. Glorify God in your suffering, "not my will God, but your will; God will help you have faith.

If you feel like giving up; just look back on how far you are already. Before you give up; think of the reason why you held on so long. We are never defeated, unless we give up on God. When we refuse to give up; the greatest tragedy of our life can actually turn out to be one of the greatest blessings. When we press on or persevere through difficulties or weariness, "we refuse to give up" on what God has called us to do.

I know it's not easy to keep doing the right thing when it feels like you're getting nothing in return. But I want to let you know: The Bible (God's

Word), promises if we will persevere, we will see a return on our investment. Our words and actions can make an eternal impact on the people around us. We might not know the legacy we left on this side of eternity but we can trust that Jesus will bless our hard work.

> James 1:12, says, *"Blessed is the one who perseveres under trial because, having stood the test, that person will receive the crown of life that the Lord has promised to those who love him."*

Yes, that person will receive the "crown of life" that the Lord has promised to those, who love him." The "crown of life" is mentioned twice in the New Testament; once in James and once in Revelations. In both instances; the "crown of life" is received by those who stand the test through perseverance in the faith. When James and John refer to the "crown of life," they are not thinking of some actual or literal, physical crown. The "crown of life" refers to eternal life itself. It's not just a bonus reward that only some people get in the eternal kingdom, but rather, the prize received by all entrants into heaven. Put in simple terms, "crown of life" means more specifically "the crown that is life." Life itself is the future reward!

God always hears us when we call on Him. He doesn't always give us what we want but He always gives us what is best for us. If we trust the Lord, even when we don't understand:

> we can begin to see where the Lord is working in our lives, whether it's experiencing His faithfulness through a financial need or His goodness through our Christian friendships that show us support and encouragement. When we ask for help and then seek God, He will open our eyes to experience Him in new ways that bring us closer to Him. God's understanding is far greater than ours and we have to trust that His timing is perfect.

We serve a mighty God who will never abandon us and who wants the best for our lives. It's not always easy to wait in a world of instant gratification or pleasure. But if we stop limiting God to our own deadlines, demands, and desires, we can experience a calmness during the chaos or confusion in our lives. One thing you can remember is; with God's help you can paddle or push your way through the confusion, and move to clarity.

> 1 Corinthians 14:33, says, *"God is not the author of confusion but of peace and whenever you feel confused, you can be sure that God is not part of it."*

The enemy creates confusion to distort the truth coming forth into your minds. Even in churches, it is wise that you test every spirit/person that prophesies to you (1 John 4). Confusion divides, separates, and destroys God's Truth from you. God is clear in everything He tells you, and he will never give you contradicting information. The confusion comes through other means and seeks to make us second guess, what God told us, in the secret place.

In conclusion, there are many reasons why we encounter confusion but we don't have to despair or be miserable because there is always a way out! Every time you get confused; turn to God's Word, which will clarify every issue that is confusing you. Even when you are confused, God is always ready to clear your mind so that you can make decisions without any doubt. God planned for us to do good things and to live as he has always wanted us to live. This is why he sent Jesus Christ to make us what we are. Whenever we have the opportunity, we have to do what is good for everyone; especially for the family of believers.

Sometimes giving up is a sign or indication that people were never true followers of Christ. John 3:3 (KJV), says, *"³Jesus answered and said unto him, Verily, verily, I say unto thee, except a man be born again, he cannot see the kingdom of God."*

Those who have truly been born again by the Spirit of God will never give Jesus up. They are kept in the Lord's hand (John 10:28–29), and they will persevere to the end. You need to persevere so that when you have done the will of God, you will receive what he has promised (Hebrews 10:36).

OUR ACTIONS WILL SHOW

Believers do not need to grow weary in doing good because God makes a promise to all believers that if they stay strong and continue to do good, believers will reap a harvest at the proper time (Galatians 6:9). Believers will reap a harvest at the proper time. A believer is one who has received the truth that Jesus Christ is the Son of God into their hearts, resulting in a new creation (John 1:12; 2 Corinthians 5:17). A believer does more than hear Jesus' words and accept what He said about God; a believer allows the information to change him (see John 2:23–24).

NOTES:

Chapter 5

LISTEN FOR THE HOLY SPIRIT'S GUIDANCE

Before Jesus ascended to heaven, He told His disciples that He would send one who would teach and guide all those who believe in Him (Acts 1:5; John 14:26; 16:7). Jesus' promise was fulfilled less than two weeks later when the Holy Spirit came in power on the believers at Pentecost (Acts 2). Now, when a person believes in Christ, the Holy Spirit immediately (or instantly) becomes a permanent part of his (or her) life (Romans 8:14; 1 Corinthians 12:13; Ephesians 1:13–14).

The Holy Spirit has many functions. Not only does He (the holy spirit) distribute spiritual gifts according to His will (1 Corinthians 12:7–11) but He also comforts us (John 14:16, KJV), and teaches us (John 14:26), and remains in us as a seal of promise upon our hearts until the day of Jesus' return (Ephesians 1:13; 4:30). The Holy Spirit also takes on the role of Guide and Counselor, leading us in the way we should go and revealing God's truth (Luke 12:12; 1 Corinthians 2:6–10).

It's important for us to listen for the Holy Spirit's guidance. In John 14:26: Jesus describes the Holy Spirit:

> *"But the Advocate, the Holy Spirit, whom the Father will send in my name, will teach you all things and will remind you of everything I have said to you."*

If we listen for the Holy Spirit's guidance, it will be easier to know what's right. Jesus glorifies the Father (God). He does it through his people as they do God's work and keeps His commandments. Apart from the power of the Holy Spirit and prayer, we could never glorify the Lord. It's one thing for us to go to heave and quite something else for heaven to come to us.

There is a deeper fellowship with the Son, Jesus Christ and the Father God for those who love Him, seek Him, and obey Him. We experience His peace and presence as we commune with the Father and the Son, in Love. Jesus is the way to the Father; He reveals the truth about the Father, and He shares the life of the Father of with us. So, why should our hearts be troubled? If a believer truly loves and obeys the Lord, he or she will experience fellowship with God. If a person does not love God; he or she will not, obey Him.

God wants a person heart, not lip service; He is not impressed with lip service. Worship God in spirit and truth.

Disobedience is a serious matter; Jesus' words are the words of God. Jesus told His disciples these things while He was with them but the Holy Spirit came; He would remind the disciples of all things that Jesus had said and would teach all things (see 1 Corinthians 2:13):

> *"This is what we speak, not in words taught us by human wisdom but in words taught by the Spirit, explaining spiritual realities with Spirit-taught words.*

This promise was primarily fulfilled through the lives of the apostles in the writing of the New Testament. Matthew and John wrote down Jesus' words. Peter wrote about the gospel in his two letters and may have dictated some of the memories of Jess to Mark. Yes, the holy spirit teaches! In 1

Corinthians 2:13, the apostle Paul, emphasized that the intellectuals of this world could not teach the knowledge he was giving to the Corinthian believers. Note that the spirit did not simply dictate words to Paul and the other apostles; he taught them.

The apostles related with their own vocabulary and style what they had learn from the spirit. I write this significant message in this chapter to help you and others to listen but also recognize the Holy Spirit's guidance. You and many others who read my book will perhaps may ask or think; Pastor Watson, how do I recognize the Holy Spirit guidance? How do I discern between my own thoughts and His leading?

The Holy Spirit does not speak with audible words; He guides us through our own consciences (Romans 9:1), and other quiet subtle ways. One of the most important ways to recognize the Holy Spirit's guidance is to be familiar with God's Word. The Bible is the ultimate source of wisdom about how we should live (2 Timothy 3:16). Believers are to search the Scriptures, meditate on them, and commit them to memory (Joshua 1:8).

_____

_____

_____

_____

_____

_____

The Word is the "sword of the Spirit" (Ephesians 6:17) and the Spirit will use it to speak to us (John 16:12–14) to reveal God's will for our lives. He (the Holy Spirit) will also bring specific Scriptures to mind at times when we need them most (John 14:26). Knowledge of God's Word can help us

LISTEN FOR THE HOLY SPIRIT'S GUIDANCE

to discern whether or not our desires come from the Holy Spirit. We must test our inclinations or our learnings against Scripture.

The Holy Spirit will never prod or poke us to do anything contrary or conflicting to God's Word. If it conflicts with the Bible, then it is not from the Holy Spirit, and should be ignored. I must reemphasize; if, it conflicts with the Bible then it is not from the Holy Spirit and should be ignored. It is also necessary for us to be in continual prayer with the Father (1 Thessalonians 5:17). Not only does this keep our hearts and minds open to the Holy Spirit's leading, but it also allows the Spirit to speak on our behalf:

_____

_____

_____

_____

_____

_____

> Romans 8:26–27, says, *"In the same way, the Spirit helps us in our weakness. We do not know what we ought to pray for, but the Spirit himself intercedes for us through wordless groans. And he who searches our hearts knows the mind of the Spirit, because the Spirit intercedes for God's people in accordance with the will of God."*

Another way to tell if we are following the Spirit's leading is to look for signs of His fruit in our lives (Galatians 5:22–23). If we walk in the Spirit, we will continue to see these qualities grow and mature in us, and they will become evident to others as well. It's important to note that we have the choice whether or not to accept the Holy Spirit's guidance. When we know

OUR ACTIONS WILL SHOW

the will of God but do not follow it; we are resisting the Spirit's work in our lives (Acts 7:51; 1 Thessalonians 5:19) and a desire to follow our own way grieves Him (the Holy Spirit) (Ephesians 4:30).

_____

_____

_____

_____

_____

_____

_____

The holy Spirit will never lead us into sin; habitual sin will cause us to miss what the Holy Spirit wants to say to us through the Word of God. Being in tune with God's will, turning from and confessing sin, and making a habit of prayer and the study of God's Word, will allow us to recognize and follow the holy Spirit's leading. I said previously; Jesus describes the Holy Spirit in John 14:26:

> *"But the Advocate, the Holy Spirit, whom the Father will send in my name, will teach you all things and will remind you of everything I have said to you."*

Jesus being our Advocate, Intercessor and Mediator: He is our Advocate with the Father, our Lord and Savior, Jesus Christ is the bridge between us and God. Thank God for His indescribable gift (2 Corinthians 9:15).

Jesus is our Advocate; He advocates for us! Jesus intercedes for us; He stands in our place. We don't get what we deserve; instead, we get grace after grace, God's Mercy, and God's unfailing, unconditional and everlasting love. The blood of Jesus speaks for me and you, but one of the questions people ask the most is: "How do I hear the Holy Spirit?" They think there must be a magic formula involved and while there is not a 1-2-3 magic formula; there are disciplines that you can implement to put yourself in the place of hearing the Holy Spirit more clearly. Remember, the Holy Spirit is always speaking; it's just a matter of us opening our spiritual ears to hear Him.

I like share three ways that I read and noted by Ms. Gloria Copeland (supported by God's Word) on how you can improve your ability to hear the Holy Spirit:

1) **Hear the Holy Spirit when you Focus on the Word:** One of the most effective ways to improve your ability to hear the Holy Spirit, is by focusing on God's Word.

   > In John 15:7, Jesus said, *"But if you remain in me and my words remain in you, you may ask for anything you want, and it will be granted."*

How do you know when you have been focusing enough on the Word? The Holy Spirit talks to you through it and directs your thoughts as you go about your day. He brings it to your mind when challenges arise, and helps you know what to do. You focus on the Word by spending time in it. You can't just read it casually every now and then. You have to be diligent (attentive) to read your Bible and reflect on it every day and obey it. treat it like the priceless treasure, it is!

2) **Hear the Holy Spirit when you Listen to God's People:** The Holy Spirit is not only speaking to you; He's speaking to all of God's people.

Sometimes those people have received a message from the Lord for the church. Just like when the Lord spoke through the Apostles. Other times, the Holy Spirit uses those people to share a special message specifically for you. By listening to trusted faith ministers and even Spirit-led friends and family members, you can hear the Holy Spirit's direction. Now, that doesn't mean you should listen to every person, or even every Christian who believes that God wants them to tell you something. Make sure those people are Holy Spirit-filled, Spirit-led and full of faith.

3) **Hear the Holy Spirit when you Listen in Prayer:** Do you find yourself doing all the talking in your prayer time with the Lord?

_____

_____

_____

_____

_____

_____

If you never get quiet enough to listen, how will you ever hear what the Holy Spirit is speaking to your heart? When you pray, spend some time praising God for His goodness and thanking Him for all He has done for you (Psalm 100:4). Then ask Him for what you need (Philippians 4:13). After that, get quiet; Prayer is not a one-way conversation. Make sure that you give the Holy Spirit a chance to speak. He may bring a scripture or song to your mind. He may bring a person to mind that needs prayer. Or, He may give you direction for your day or even an answer for a prayer request.

Keeping a prayer journal is another great way to identify the Holy Spirit's voice. Write-down what you've asked the Lord for and the different ways He has answered those prayers. Write the thoughts He brings to your mind. As you put this into practice, you will begin to understand how the Holy Spirit works in and through you. You will begin to hear and read His answers.

LISTEN FOR THE HOLY SPIRIT'S GUIDANCE

In conclusion, the Holy Spirit is talking; it's up to you, to hear Him clearly. By putting the three keys or three ways below on how you can improve your ability to hear the Holy Spirit:

1) Hear the Holy Spirit when you Focus on the Word.
2) Hear the Holy Spirit when you Listen to God's People.
3) Hear the Holy Spirit when you Listen in Prayer

_____

_____

_____

_____

_____

_____

_____

You will improve your ability to hear the Holy Spirit, and you will have the joy of living a Spirit-led life! Listen for the Holy Spirit's guidance; He will speak to your heart. Trust me, the Holy Spirit will not contradict the Bible.

NOTES:

Chapter 6

KNOW THE SPIRIT OF TRUTH AND ERROR

14 But people who aren't spiritual[a] can't receive these truths from God's Spirit. It all sounds foolish to them and they can't understand it, for only those who are spiritual can understand what the Spirit means (1 Corinthians 2:14; NLT).

The Spirit of truth; the world cannot accept God because it neither sees Him, nor knows Him. But you know Him for He lives with you and will be in you. *"Whoever belongs to God hears what God says. The reason you do not hear is that you do not belong to God."* (John 8:47)

Just Take a look around the world, we live in; whose truth would you say is being followed; Satan's or God's? It is evident that we live in a broken world. But that does not cancel or remove our ability to recognize and utilize God's truth, and authority in guiding our choices and lifestyle. With God's truth and the Holy Spirit, spiritual discernment is possible. Without God's truth and the Holy Spirit, spiritual discernment is impossible; please thoroughly read 1 Corinthians 2:14-15 (NKJV):

"14 But the natural man does not receive the things of the Spirit of God, for they are foolishness to him; nor can he know them, because

> *they are spiritually discerned. ⁱ⁵But he who is spiritual judges all things, yet he himself is rightly judged by no one."*

When we choose to disregard the authority of Scripture, and the leading of the Holy Spirit, we are inviting chaos and disorder into the world. We become willing participants in Satan's plans. But Spiritual discernment is the ability to recognize and use God's truth and authority to guide our life.

God's Word and His Spirit is the "standard for truth" and help us to identify error and deception. Refusing to listen to God is the ultimate foolishness; since it ends in our own harm. May we all listen carefully to God's Word, and be one, with His word.

> First John 4:5–6, says, *"⁵They are from the world; THEREFORE, they speak from the world, and the world listens to them. ⁶We are from God. Whoever knows God listens to us; whoever is not from God does not listen to us. By this we know the Spirit of truth and the spirit of error."*

The Holy Spirit is called, "The Spirit of Truth. The Holy Spirit is called "The Spirit of Truth" because our connection with Him is what enables us to obey the command of 1 Timothy 2:15:

> *"Do your best to present yourself to God as one approved, a worker who has no need to be ashamed, rightly handling the word of truth."*

The Apostle Paul desired to excel in everything He did for the Lord (2 Timothy 2:15). So, he tackled his God assigned mission to preach the gospel with all-out fervor giving himself entirely to the work of the Lord. He warmly encouraged fellow believers to do the same:

> *"Therefore, my beloved brothers, be steadfast, immovable, always abounding in the work of the Lord, knowing that in the Lord your labor is not in vain"* (1 Corinthians 15:58, ESV).

The Holy Spirit gives believers the power to live like Jesus and be bold witnesses for Him. The disciples of Jesus, both then and now are not expected to figure everything out on their own. Instead, they will be guided by the Helper. We will experience His guidance minute-by-minute as he applies God's Word to our hearts and lives. God's Holy Spirit, is "the Spirit of Truth. When the Spirit Speaks Truth to You; the Spirit Brings glory to Jesus. There are many ways the Holy Spirit works in the lives of Christians but they all share one common goal: to make us more like Jesus Christ.

The Holy Spirit works in believers by renewing our minds to be like the mind of Christ. He does this by convicting us of sin and leading us to repentance. Through repentance; the Holy Spirit wipes out what was dirty in us and allows us to bear good fruit. As we allow the Holy Spirit to continue nourishing that fruit, we grow to be like or resemble, Jesus Christ more. Glory hallelujah!

In 1 John 4:5–6, John suggests that there are forces of spiritual darkness that guide and influence the world (4:5-6). The comparison or the difference between those in the world and those who are of God. They are of the world; therefore, they speak as of the world, and the world hears them. We are of God; He who knows God, hears us; he who is not of God, does not hear us.

John 15:19 (NKJV), says:

> *"If you were of the world, the world would love its own. Yet because you are not of the world, but I chose you out of the world, therefore the world hates you."*

We all have haters; trust me! I don't lose any sleep concerning, my haters... Why? God's word says, in Luke 6:22, *"Blessed are you when people hate you, when they exclude you and insult you and reject your name as evil, because of the Son of Man (Jesus Christ)."*

OUR ACTIONS WILL SHOW

The unbelieving world prefers selfishness and pleasure, over honoring God. In 1 John 5:19, the apostle draws the comparison: We know that we are of God, and the whole world lies in the power of the evil one (Satan). Naturally, if you were to go out and ask people on the street, "Do you hate Jesus Christ?" Most would answer, "No, I don't have anything against Jesus; He was a great moral teacher." If you asked, "Do you follow the devil" they would strongly or ADAMANTLY, yell or shout:

> "There's no way that I follow the devil! I'm not a Satan-worshiper!" Let's keep it real or keep it 100! They don't follow Jesus, but they are not openly opposed, or in opposition to Him, either. And they are not aware that they are following the devil, even though they actually are. They subscribe to godless values. They ignore God in their daily lives, unless they get into a crisis or trouble where they, all of a sudden, pray.

The average unbeliever is not going to say, "I hate Jesus, and I hate Christians!" I said, the average unbeliever is not going to say, "I hate Jesus and I hate Christians!" He's just living his life as he sees fit and is content or satisfied to let the believing people follow Jesus, if they want to. When "the Spirit of truth" comes; He will guide you into all the truth. He will not speak on His own, but He will speak whatever He hears. He will also declare to you, what is to come. The Holy Spirit is always speaking. It's just a matter of opening your spiritual ears, to hear Him.

Focus on the Word; one of the most effective ways to improve your ability to hear the Holy Spirit is by focusing on the Word of God. The Holy Spirit lives inside us when we accept Jesus Christ and helps us grow closer to God. The moment we receive Christ as our lord and Savior, the Holy Spirit comes to live in our hearts. The Bible teaches that the Holy Spirit is all-powerful, and present everywhere. Anyone who belongs to God listens gladly to the words of God. But one does not listen because he or she does not belong to God.

Sometimes, we may not feel qualified to do God's will, but His holy Spirit within us provides all we need. The Holy Spirit guides us in our spirits (not through our physical body). The Holy Spirit helps us in our weakness. For example, we don't know what God wants us to pray for. But the Holy Spirit prays for us with groanings that cannot be expressed in words. God says in His Word:

> *"A time will come when people will not listen to accurate teachings. Instead, they will follow their own desires and surround themselves with teachers who tell them what they want to hear."* (2 Timothy 4:3)

Jesus Christ never sugar-coated the truth; He did not preach a sugar-coated message. He declared that devil is the father of those who do not believe in His Word and follow the desires of the devil and sin. All preachers and teachers of the gospel need to break-down, rather than sugar-coating or watering-down, the truth of God's Word. Many preachers and teachers have sugar- coated or watered the Gospel down, reducing it to merely a message of escape from condemnation, without repenting from sin.

The one who belongs to God, listens to His word; if you don't listen to God's Word, it's because you don't belong to Him. Listening involves both hearing and doing God's word: God wants us to carefully pay attention so that we can fully obey. Listening is synonymous with obedience in Jeremiah:

> *"I spoke to you in your prosperity, but you said, 'I will not listen.' This has been your way from your youth, that you have not obeyed my voice"* (Jeremaih 22:21).

This is how many people "listen" to God's Word: They listen and willing to hear God's Word, but they are not willing to obey when it is inconvenient or undesirable. Instead, they look for every possible excuse to make things difficult and water the plain voice of God, in Scripture. God is patient with those who do not listen, but his patience eventually runs out. Refusing to listen to God is the worst kind of stubbornness and the ultimate foolishness, since it ends in our own harm: certain judgment by the hand of the Almighty.

In conclusion, God wants everyone to hear His truth but many will not or no longer listen. Just look around and see what's happening today in this world. Don't wander off after man-made rules or fictions, or untruths; you, stand firm in God's Word in all that you do.

> First John 4:1, says, *"Beloved, do not believe every spirit, but test the spirits to see whether they are from God, because many false prophets have gone out into the world."*

John Chapter 4; includes two major sections: in the first section, John briefly instructs believers to examine spiritual claims, since not every teacher is loyal to the truth. Verse 1: explains what we are to do: test! It also explains why: The presence of false teachers. Verses 2 through 6: address how we are to test, in order to determine whether the spirits are from God. The use of the term "spirit," in this case or situation; is not a reference to ghosts, demons, or other creatures. Rather, this is a reference to the attitude and approach of a particular teacher. In reality, truth only comes from the Holy Spirit; everything else comes from evil. The reason for John's warning is given next. Believers will face false prophets, because there are quite a few in the world. If this was a problem when John wrote his letter many centuries ago, it's even more of an issue today. Therefore, it's important to have a way to test which teachers and leaders are from God. Verses 2 through 6 give details related to the difference between true and false teachers; false teachers distort or twist what Jesus taught. It's important to remember Jesus' words from John 8:31-32:

> *"If you hold to my teaching, you are really my disciples. Then you will know the truth, and the truth will set you free."*

If you don't know the truth; you can't be free. So logically, people who believe a lie are being kept in bondage. It's important to know The Spirit of Truth, and the spirit of error thru spiritual discernment.

NOTES:

Chapter 7

SHOW YOUR BEST CHARACTER AND CONDUCT

It's important to show our best Character and Conduct as followers and believers in Christ Jesus. People of character are well-known for their honesty, ethics, and charity or kindness. Descriptions such as "man of principle" and "woman of integrity" are assertions of character. A lack of character is moral deficiency, and people lacking character tend to behave dishonestly, unethically, and uncharitably or unkindly. Character is influenced and developed by our choices. Character, in turn, influences our choices. We can develop character by controlling our thoughts, practicing Christian virtues, guarding our heart, and keeping, good company. Men and women of character will set a good example for others to follow, and their godly reputation will be evident to all.

> Proverbs 17:25, states that *"A foolish son brings grief to his father and bitterness to the mother who bore him."*

Foolishness describes a state of mind and a matter of character. Stay with me, I'm going somewhere with this; there is no way to put into numbers or percentages how much, a parent loves a child. Not only do they give life to their children, but they raise them, provide them with guidance, help them overcome obstacles, give of themselves and love them unconditionally.

As children; we often forget how much our parents have done for us, in our lives. But taking a second to really think of their love and support, can help build bonds of love and respect. Recognize when parents seem to be getting in your way; they are but with good reason. Parents often act as a shield or guard to protect their children from anything that they consider to be harmful. Why? Because parents love their children, and they are concerned about their children's or grandchildren's well-being and future success. When parents see or perceive their children's behavior as something that threatens to limit their potential achievement or success; it can often cause conflict in your relationship. But please realize it usually comes from a place of love.

Sometimes, it may seem like our parents don't understand and that can lead to a negative relationship with them. Regardless of that, it is important to remain respectful toward your parents. If you want to show your parents more respect you can easily reevaluate or reconsider your thoughts and actions towards your parents. Do this to ensure that you are treating them with the kindness they deserve. Don't turn your back on your parents, don't turn your back on your family because you will reap what you sow.

Disrespectful and disobedient children are becoming more, more common these days. Not my opinion, or anyone else's opinion. Disrespectful children are not a credit to anyone (Proverbs 17:25), including themselves. The Bible has much to say about them (Disrespectful and disobedient children). Proverbs 17:25, is a verse or scripture that says, *"a foolish son causes sorrow (grief) and bitterness to his parents."* Obviously, a wise son brings joy to his mother, as well as to his father, and a foolish son grieves his father as well as his mother.

The use of "father" in one line and "mother" in the next, is simply a common construction in well-known or proverbial literature. Both parents experience either joy or sorrow depending on their son's behavior. We were taught early in life, not to talk back (back-talk) to our parents; talking back to your parents, was a no, no, and you would reap the consequences. Talking back (or back-talk) to your parents, is very disrespectful. Backtalk is a disrespectful response to a parent in the form of yelling, cursing, eye rolling, or even sarcasm (you know; the smart remarks). Backtalk or talking back occurs as a way to fight back, but all it does is create conflict. Learning to manage unthinking or thoughtless reactions helps to show parents that you respect their authority.

As a parent, if you aren't the boss in your family; the lines of authority can become confused or cloudy very quickly. When your children are uncertain about who's really in charge, they often act out, engage in risky behavior, or become extremely bossy and demeaning or full of themselves, as a result. And eventually, you start to resent your own child because you don't have a way to tell them, what to do. You have effectively, lost control.

Many parents also want to be their child's friend; they don't like the idea of being the boss at all. The major problem with this approach is that a friend is non-judgmental, and a friend is a peer (your child's equal). Parents your child's role simply is not equal to yours, as a parent. You have to make judgments and be in charge because otherwise, no one will be in charge.

The majority of our communication comes from not what we say, but how we say it. It's in the tone of your voice, your eye contact, and the way you move. Be sure that your non-verbal signals demonstrate respect and understanding. Sometimes as parents, we may ask ourselves, where did I go wrong? When a child does something horribly or terribly wrong, it's typical for parents to ask themselves; "Where did we go wrong?" You start wondering or re-live memories, where things could have possibly contributed to a child's downfall or disgrace.

A time where discretion failed or parental mistakes were made. You think back on how you could have done things differently, if given the chance. But the truth is, we are not perfect parents because we are not perfect people. The Bible is very clear that "all" have fallen short of the glory of God. (Roman 3:23). Did we mess up or made mistakes sometime during our children's childhood or raising them? Yes, of course we did, we all mess up or messed-up, somehow. God did not call us to be perfect parents. Why would he; knowing what he has to work with? We are painfully flawed (we, are not perfect!). Parents, please stop beating yourselves up!

Parents, we could not raise a child perfectly, no matter how hard we try because we cannot even conceive in our hearts what perfect, really is! Romans 3:10, *"tells us that "there is no one righteous, not even one."* That's right, not even one! That's why Jesus Christ came; not so you could raise a child perfectly, so that in your failure to parent perfectly, He would reconcile, what is lost and fallen. If you parented or raised your children perfectly, Jesus, wouldn't have needed to come; and parenting is not all he needed to save.

Jesus came to save marriages, churches, families, the world, me, and you. The other truth to realize is, your child is not perfect either. Even when there were instances where you did things well, he or she can respond righteously or in sin. Our child or children gets to choose. Every human being is created in the image of God (Genesis 1:27; James 3:9). Part of what it means to be in God's image is: we have a conscience (a sense of right and wrong) that instinctively recognizes good and evil, and tells right from wrong. Due to our sin nature; we tend to excuse the evil in ourselves (Romans 5:12; Proverbs 20:20; Jeremiah 2:35).

Your child, gets to choose.

A great example; you might help your son or daughter get a driver's license by investing risk, your life, time, and money to make sure it's done properly to give him/her the best possible end result or outcome. Afterwards, He/she then might choose his/her newfound freedom to drive to church events, or take food to the shut-in, or he/she might use it to attend the latest drinking party or sneak around to attend something dangerous or very risky. So, even if it was possible for your child to have the perfect parent; your child can still choose to be imperfect and sin.

> Psalm 51:5, says, *"Surely I was sinful at birth, sinful from the time my mother conceived me."*

OUR ACTIONS WILL SHOW

We are born in sin because mankind is fallen. Your child needs a Savior just as much as you do, and you are not it. You see, perfection is not something we humans practice on this side of eternity. Our brain knows that it should exist and at one time it did, but we chose death. So, in answer to the original question, "Where did I go wrong? It happened in the garden!!! But the better question is, "Where did I go, right?" The answer is, "I told my children about a God who loves, and sent His Son to die for their sins, and mine."

How much pain do you cause your parents? How much will your children, cause you pain? Solomon observed this calamity or disaster in families, where a foolish child can cause both parents great pain. The lessons are simple; obey and honor your parents, and train your children. Godly parents know this proverb is true. Fathers grieve when children are foolish, and mothers are pained seeing them reject wisdom for folly (foolishness). Worldly parents are not as troubled because they do not understand wisdom, nor do they recognize foolish children. Mothers endure pain bringing their children into the world and they work hard and long bringing those children to maturity. But if the parents neglect training them in the way of the Lord, those children can bring far greater grief and bitterness in the future than childbirth or thankless years doing laundry.

After obeying and honoring parents, you should choose a godly and wise lifestyle dedicated to righteousness and truth. Your highest reasons to do so should be God's glory and serving His kingdom on earth. But before you consider your own prosperity and pleasure under God's blessing for such a life, you should consider "showing your parents the best character and conduct" for their great peace and pleasure. Show Your best Character and Conduct!

In conclusion, child training, requiring sacrifice and investment has a fabulous return for all parties. It will save you from the grief and bitterness described in this chapter. It will bring joy and pleasure to see children living godly and productive lives. It will also bring prosperity and success to your children, and you will please the God who loaned your children to you.

If you train your children when they are young, they will give you pleasure when they are old, by walking in the ways you know are good (Proverbs 22:6). God loaned them to you with foolishness bound in them, but He has told you how to drive it far away (Proverbs 19:18; 22:15; 23:13-14). Fathers, training is not an option (Ephesians 6:4). And mothers, you must participate as well (Proverbs 1:8; 6:20).

The choice is up to you, but the consequences are certain. If you trained your child, and you have a fool, he will bear his own burden (Galatians 6:5). There have never been perfect parents, and God knows it. The Bible says, "children who are not disciplined or who fail to obey their parents are much worse off in life (see Proverbs 22:15; 19:18; and 29:15).

NOTES:

Chapter 8

GOTTA KEEP MOVING FORWARD

We, as people or children of God, must "keep moving forward, no matter what! It's only in moving forward; we can accomplish what God has called us to do. The temptation to look back will be great, but we must let go of the old, and reach for the new. We should not want to remain stuck in any area of our lives, and we cannot live life in reverse or backwards.

Life can only be understood backwards; but it must be lived forward. God doesn't want us to look back because dwelling on the past, can hinder our spiritual growth, and prevent us from moving forward in our relationship with him (God).

> *"The righteous keep moving forward, and those with clean hands become stronger and stronger"* (Job 17:9).

God wants you to move forward and not look backward. God specializes in healing, making us whole, and making everything work out for our good. Sometimes moving forward may require changing jobs, transferring or moving to a new city or state, or walk away from something or somebody as we reach for something different. Yes, I realize embracing change is not always easy but it's best when the change results from something positive in our lives, such as; getting married, a promotion, buying a new house, or new car.

Sometimes, change means walking away from bad situations or poor choices. I'm sure many have made some bad choices, or in bad situations, and that had to be walked away from.

The Bible speaks to the issue of walking away from conflict in a number of passages or scriptures. Jesus taught us that it is sometimes better to turn the other cheek (in Matthew 5:39); He also told us to go the extra mile, even when we don't feel like it (Matthew 5:41). Walk away from the evil things in the world; just leave them behind, and do what is right, and always seek peace and pursue it.

Sometimes when bad things happen, we think that it's fate, or that's the end. We think that God destined us for these bad things which lead to anger. Yet, it's not necessarily that God destined us for bad things. We will experience change as we learn to trust God properly: To truly walk with God, we must be willing to grow. We advance and go from glory to glory (2 Corinthians 3:18) which means we continually change into who God created us to be. As we become closer to God, we begin to live closer to the example that Jesus showed us.

In Job 17:9, Job reflects upon the harsh criticism or condemnation his friends had passed upon him, and, Job looking on himself as a dying man; he appeals or pleas to God. It concerns us carefully to redeem the days of time and to spend them in being ready for eternity. When we move forward with God, we cannot expect everyone to understand our choices. We cannot make decisions based on whether or not we gain their approval. We don't need their approval.

Some friends may not understand the idea. When family and friends do not support our desire to change, it may be hard for us to accept that they do not, support our desire to change. But we must not seek to live solely or just for the approval or praise of others.

> Galatians 1:10, says, *"Am I now trying to win the approval of human beings, or God? Or am I trying to please people? If I were still trying to please people, I would not be a servant of Christ."*

Job suffered tremendously and endured his trials with patience. However, while he was going through his darkest days, three of his friends arrived to "comfort him" (Job 2:11). They turned out to be "miserable comforters," in Job's estimation (Job 16:2). They only added to his pain. Job's would-be comforters offered all sorts of possibilities for why Job was going through such misery, but adding insult to injury, they focused on the theory that Job must have unconfessed sin in his life and that God was punishing him (Job 11:14–15; 22:4–7). Knowing his conscience was clear; Job grew weary of his so-called three friends' accusations and blurted out, "I have heard many things like these; you are miserable comforters, all of you" (Job 16:2). If the situation were reversed, Job would have spoken words of strength and help to them in their suffering.

Let me ask you; do your words wear others out or encourage them? Do you add to their pain or suffering? Job was wronged or mistreated by his comforters, their harsh words tormented him, broke him, and criticized or condemned him. Job had expressed hope that God would vindicate him even after death, but his hope was almost gone.

Since job brought up the matter of death and the grave, Bildad decided to elaborate on the subject. Bildad, is one of the three principal or primary comforters of Job (Job 2:11). He painted some vivid pictures of the death of the wicked: it is like a light, put out; it is like an animal trapped; it is like a criminal pursued, and it is like a tree rooted up!

Job seemed wronged by God; why should one sinner receive so much punishment? Bildad's description of death in Job, chapter 18 was Job's description of his life (vv. 7-12):

> "He was a living dead man," and his hope was gone! To make things even worst; job was wronged by his family and friends.

OUR ACTIONS WILL SHOW

Those closest to him, stayed farthest from him, and those who should have shown him respect only mocked him. Job was a lonely man crying out for pity, but nobody, answered. All Job saw in his future was a decaying body, death, and the grave. Once again, Job cried out for a representative before God; somebody who would put up security for him, and get his case settled.

Ask God to help you be sensitive to the cries of those who hurt, no matter what others may do. Jesus is the Advocate and Mediator for His people and their hope. He gave His own blood as security, and those who trust Him. Jesus gave His own blood as security, and those who trust Him, always have living hope. Job still had faith in God! If he died, he would see God, and one day, He would have a new body from God. This gives great confidence to God's people.

Job 17:9, says, *"The righteous keep moving forward, "and those with clean hands become stronger and stronger."*

We all need to know and understand that we can have "clean hands" when we turn from sin and follow Jesus. We cannot achieve cleanliness on our own. Only through the grace of God and His magnificent mercy and generous love can we be remade and washed of our sins. In the Bible, cleanliness means being pure, spotless, without blemish, in its perfect original and God-designed righteous state. Something can become "unclean" by being defiled or corrupted. But to become clean means to restore something to its natural and innocent state. From a moral perspective, this equates to righteousness or walking in a just and upright manner with the Lord.

Since believers are engaged in an ongoing spiritual battle with the powers of darkness, they cannot endure or persist without the power of God. To be strong in the Lord and the power of His might is vital to living a victorious Christian life. When we have clean hands, we become stronger and stronger." The believer's empowerment comes from being in Jesus.

The Lord equips us for ongoing spiritual warfare with the full armor of God! Often, we are strongest in the Lord when we operate in the realm of human weakness. When we are weak in ourselves, we are strong in the Lord because God's strength becomes evident: "Jesus was crucified in weakness, but He lives by the power of God. We are strongest because of our, spiritual union with Jesus Christ.

In conclusion, instead of following the example of Job's friends; we can truly comfort those who are suffering by assuring them that God knows what they are going through, and He cares about them (Psalm 34:18). We can remind them, as painful their situation is; God promises to use it for good in their lives if they love Him and trust Him with it (Romans 8:28).

Trying to assign blame during a time of loss can turn us into "miserable comforters." Sometimes the greatest comfort we can give a hurting friend is our quiet presence. Sometimes, as Job's friends should have learned, the best thing to say is nothing at all. Many of us want to trust God When times are good, it can feel easier. But when times feel difficult; it is even more important to trust God. Perhaps God is letting somebody go through an impossible situation right now. We must never blame God for the situation of pain, sorrow, or grief that we may endure due to someone actions, words, or evil intent towards us.

How you talk to yourself about events, experiences and people, plays a large role in shaping how you interpret or understand events. God tells you to do something, directs which steps you're to take, warns you that there will be trials, and admonishes you to take heed that the devil doesn't devour you (1 Peter 5:8). God already knows you're going to be in over your head but tells you to "keep moving forward!" Anyway!

NOTES:

Chapter 9

KNOW GOD'S WILL FOR YOUR LIFE

"Obey them not only to win their favor when their eye is on you, but as slaves of Christ, doing the will of God from your heart." (Ephesians 6:6)

Knowing the will of God is one of the most important things we can seek or pursue in our walk with the Lord. God's ultimate will for us is always to glorify Him, and help us grow spiritually. So, it's very important to know God's will. Jesus said that His true relations are those who know and do the Father's will:

"Whoever does God's will is my brother and sister and mother" (Mark 3:35).

The will of God is to repent of our sin and trust in Christ. If we have not taken that first step, then we have not yet accepted God's will. Because once we receive Christ by faith; we are made God's children. Being children of God means we have been born, into God's family. As children of God, we have a new nature "created to be like God in true righteousness and holiness" (Ephesians 4:24).

OUR ACTIONS WILL SHOW

Children of the devil (see John 8:44) make a practice of sinning but Jesus came to destroy the works of the devil in the lives of God's children (1 John 3:8). As the children of God; we are new creations in Christ (2 Corinthians 5:17), led by the Holy Spirit: *"For all who are led by the Spirit of God are children of God"* (Romans 8:14, NLT).

I stated previously, Jesus said that His true relations are those who know and do the Father's will. As we seek God's will; we should make sure what we are considering is not something the Bible forbids or prohibits. I understand wanting to Know God's will, can be sometimes difficult, because it requires patience. It's natural to want to know all of God's will at once, but that's not how God usually works. God reveals to us a step at a time; each move a step of faith, and allows us to continue to trust God. The important thing is: as we wait for further direction; we are busy doing the good that we know to do (James 4:17).

Oftentimes, we want God to give us specifics (details): where to work, where to live, whom to marry, what car to buy, etc. God allows us to make choices, and, if we are yielded (surrendered) to Him; He has ways of preventing wrong choices; see Acts 16:6–7 below:

> *"⁶And they went through the region of Phrygia and Galatia, having been forbidden by the Holy Spirit to speak the word in Asia. ⁷And when they had come up to Mysia, they attempted to go into Bithynia, but the Spirit of Jesus did not allow them."*

Get this; they (apostle Paul and Tim) passed by Mysia, and went down to Troas; they are controlled not by the flesh, but by the holy Spirit that lives in them. If anyone does not have the Spirit of Christ, he does not belong to Christ (Galatians 4:6). He does not belong to Christ, not by way of eyeservice, as men-pleasers, but as slaves of Christ, doing the will of God from the heart (Hebrews 10:7).

To know God's will, is the highest of all wisdom! Living in the center of God's will, rules out all falseness or deception of religion, and puts the stamp of true genuineness or realness upon our service to God. The Bible instructs us to do the will of God from the heart (Ephesians 6:6). God's Spirit opens the eyes of our heart, and what was once boring, ridiculous, foolish, or unreal; is now self-evidently real. Our true self, inside of us; is evident.

If we are walking closely with the Lord and truly desiring His will for our lives, God will place His desires in our hearts. The key is wanting God's will, not our own.

> *"Delight yourself in the LORD and He will give you the desires of your heart" (Psalm 37:4).*

But as slaves of Christ, doing the will of God from your heart." What it means to be a slave of Christ is to be abiding with Christ like the slaves used to abide or live with their master. It means we submit our will to God's will. It means we own nothing except that which God has given us (1 Corinthians 4:7). It means we are God's possessions! It's not as if we have a choice in the matter.

Slaves are at the whim or urge of the owner and not in control of their own lives. One good thing about being a slave of Christ is: we are no longer slaves to sin or in bondage to sin. We were dead in our sins anyway, without even realizing it (Ephesians 2:1-2). This is why we must die to ourselves and live for Christ! We live for Him because we are owned by Him, and whatever he desires should be whatever we desire. That's because a slave knows his master better than a servant does, and the rewards for slave are infinitely or substantially greater than just being a servant.

To know God's will for your life, you must walk with God; surrender your will to God's will, obey God's commands, seek God's wisdom, seek God's kingdom, be patient, trust God, and seek his guidance through prayer. God doesn't just speak in big, life-changing moments. He's also in the little details of our day-to-day lives. So, keep an eye out for those moments or opportunities that feel like they might be nudges or pushes from God.

OUR ACTIONS WILL SHOW

Knowing and doing God's will is largely a matter of knowing His Word and walking in it. If you don't know God's will; perhaps you're thinking or wondering right now, "what is the will of God for my life?" Let me help you; to know, the will of God, for your life:

1) Learn how to walk with God, surrender your will.
2) Obey God's Word, seek godly input, pay attention to your gifts, listen to His Spirit, and be willing to change!

Before God will begin to reveal His will to you. You must be committed to doing whatever it is that He desires for you to do. God will likely be slow to show you His plan, if He knows you will likely not do that plan anyway. Many people seem to want to know what God's plan is for their lives, but they overlook the fact that 98% of God's will is already presented or explained carefully through His Word.

God is very clear about many aspects of His will. For instance, it is clearly His plan that we abstain from sexual immorality (1 Thessalonians 4:3). If we do not obey the things that God has shown us clearly to be His will; why would we think God would reveal any further information regarding His plan for our lives? Obedience, is an important first step.

In conclusion, Doing God's will, is living according to His Word (the Bible). God's will, is the highest of all wisdom. The will of God includes everything that God desires or wishes to happen in heaven and on earth. If you are interested in knowing God's will and plan for your life; you must learn to walk with God. You need to develop a personal relationship with Him.

Christianity is all about relationship rather than just religion. You will cultivate a personal relationship with the Lord best by spending time in His Word, taking time for prayer. And taking every opportunity you can to be involved in church and small group Bible study opportunities. When you seek these disciplines in your life, God will reveal His will and plan for your life.

NOTES:

Chapter 10

BEING BUSY IS NO EXCUSE

"But seek first the kingdom of God and his righteousness, and all these things will be added to you." (Matthew 6:33)

Spending time alone with God frees or clears our minds of distraction so we can focus on Him and hear His Word. Abiding in God, we enjoy the intimacy or closeness to which He calls us, and come to truly know Him. Spending time with God does not always have to be a huge time commitment. Specifically, we may start out by committing a few minutes each day of our time to reading the Bible and prayer. As we form strong habits, we can change our commitments, extend our quiet time, and add other activities to deepen our faith, such as joining a small group like; bible study. It's very important to always make time for God. We are in control of our own time given to us by God; we need to use it very wisely.

We must always make time for God; there are no excuses for not spending time with the Lord. We have time to scroll through social media or watch Netflix, but when it comes to reading our Bible or spending quiet time with God, we are suddenly "too busy. Being too busy is no excuse! We can pray when we're walking, put on worship music in our car while driving or parked, or read our bible before bed. We can always find and make time to spend with the Lord.

Spending time with God is a very important part of being a genuine believer (Christian). Christianity is less about religion and rules, and more about our personal relationship with God. Yes, life can get pretty busy, and spending time with God can seem difficult or almost impossible. But if our faith is a priority to us, then we will, make time for God.

Whether you are new to the Kingdom of God, or you have been a believer for many, many years, it is very easy to fall into the habit of forgetting to spend time with Jesus on a daily basis. But being busy or too busy, is not an excuse. We choose what we want to do with our time given to us by God. We can always find time to spend with the Lord.

Spending time with God, whether it's in church, reading our Bible, through a quick two-minute prayer, or simply in our day-to-day life, is something we as Christians, are called to do. To spend time with God means to take intentional or deliberate time out of our day to come before God through prayer, worship, and reading of the scriptures. It is a time when we draw near to God and He draws near to us, as we fellowship with Him.

But is it a requirement to put aside time for God? Is it included in our responsibilities as Christians? The Bible is full of helpful verses about spending time with God. Some Bible verses about making time for God are as follows:

> Psalm 145:18; Matthew 6:33; 1 Chronicles 16:11; Hebrews 10:24-25; Matthew 14:23; Psalm 62:8; Mark 1:35; Philippians 4:6; 2 Corinthians 6:2; Ecclesiastes 3:1-2; John 4:24; Exodus 23:25; John 1:1; Joshua 1:8; and 2 Timothy 3:16-17.

Although you might not always realize it; attending or going to church is another important part of building your personal relationship with God. Engaging or involving yourself in a community with other like-minded Christians, helps you to learn more about God, our Heavenly Father.

> In conclusion, Psalm 46:10 (NIV) *says, "Be still, and know that I am God; I will be exalted among the nations, I will be exalted in the earth."*

There is a direct link between being still and knowing that God, truly is God. If we are too busy for God, our stillness before the Lord will vanish, along with our peace. The sinful nature, the world, and Satan thrive (flourish) when we are too busy for God. The Bible says, therefore, that if you want to know God, then you must avoid busyness.

When busyness sets in and the troubles of the world begin to weigh on the human mind, the things we forget first in our memory are the things of heaven. Earth and its worries always try to crowd out God and his care (Matthew 6:25-34). The busier we are, the faster we forget about God. Busyness may make us feel important in our worldly settings, but all it's really doing is taking time away from prayer, Bible study, and our personal intimacy with God.

NOTES:

Chapter 11

WE MUST BE DOERS OF THE WORD

God wants our hearts, not lip service. There is a difference between honoring the Lord with our lips and honoring Him with our hearts. The blessing is in the doing; only doers of the Word are truly blessed, but even more blessed are all who hear the Word of God and put it into practice. We are saved by faith, in Jesus Christ, alone. We don't do good things to make God find favor in us. Furthermore, our good deeds are filthy rags when compared to God's righteousness. However, after we believe; God wants us to do many good things. He wants us to be doers of his Word. Blessing, is in the doing. The blessed hearer and doer applies the Word of God, so that it changes his/her conduct and character in the sight of God.

Is that scripture? Yes, Jesus said that only doers of the Word are truly blessed: *"But even more blessed are all who hear the word of God and put it into practice"* (Luke 11:28, NLT). I also recommend reading Matthew 15:8 and Matthew 7:21-23.

We must be doers of the Word because we are God's masterpiece created anew in Christ Jesus and He prepared good things for us to do (Ephesians 2:10). Staying active in these good works will keep us from becoming lukewarm (half-hearted). So, we should always fan into flames, the spiritual gifts, God has given us, and follow the second greatest commandment which is to "love thy neighbor." Being a doer of the Word, makes God's Word visible to other people. So, we should never grow tired of doing what, is good! Trust me, It's hard work, but its good work!

> James 1:22-25 (NKJV), says, *²²But be doers of the word, and not hearers only, deceiving yourselves. ²³For if anyone is a hearer of the word and not a doer, he is like a man observing his natural face in a mirror; ²⁴for he observes himself, goes away, and immediately forgets what kind of man he was. ²⁵But he who looks into the perfect law of liberty and continues in it, and is not a forgetful hearer but a doer of the work, this one will be blessed in what he does."*

James tells us not to just listen to God's Word. We must do what it says, or else we are only fooling ourselves. This scripture is in the middle of a passage entitled "Listening and Doing" (James 1:19-25). The passage begins by telling us we should be quick to listen, slow to speak, and slow to get angry because human anger is not, typically productive. It often causes more harm than good.

Then we should take in God's Word because it can save our souls. And then we take action, and follow what God's Word says, to do. Jesus also told us to be a doer of the Word when He said, "All who love me will do what I say. My Father will love them, and we will come and make our home with each of them" (John 14:23). And Jesus also said in Luke 11:28, *"But even more blessed are all who hear the Word of God and put it into practice."*

Whatever you have learned, received or heard from God's Word, put it into practice. The Word of God has been implanted in the believer's heart, should be received with meekness. We must be humble with a teachable spirit. We must first have a teachable spirit, ourselves, before we can teach others. Above all other learning, the Bible doctrines require a teachable spirit. If you truly desire the truth, ask the LORD every day in prayer to give you a teachable spirit. A teachable spirit is a heart ready to apply what is learnt, abandoning or forsaking the old. We don't know it all (this includes me as well), and we should not act like, we know it all, either. Because we don't! A teachable spirit is one of the most desirable and key character traits for success with God and men. The first step to learning is admitting we do not know everything. That attitude helps us with subjects at school, with marriage, at work, in the military, parenting, and with God's Word, etc.

God says, He will instruct those whose hearts are humble. Those who have a teachable spirit, who know how little they know, and how much they need to learn. He also teaches those who fear Him; those who reverence and stand in awe of Him. God has much to teach us in this life, so one must leave his or her un-teachable attitude, behind. God will teach us through His Word, through creation, through life experiences, and through the people that we meet each day.

Developing a teachable spirit will help us to delight, in life-long learning. A teachable spirit is necessary to grow and prosper in any life role or opportunity. The goal or object of teaching in the Bible, is truth and wisdom, and their related terms. James 1:22-24 (NKJV), says: *"23For if anyone is a hearer of the word and not a doer, he is like a man observing his natural face in a mirror; 24for he observes himself, goes away, and immediately forgets what kind of man he was."*

James stresses or emphases, the need to act (practice) on what we hear from God's Word. James is keeping it real; he says, we are fooling ourselves, if we think, we can be hearers only, and not doers of the Word. People who truly love God are those who keep His commands (John 14:15; 1 John 5:2–3). God desires those who hear His Word to become authentic (real, not fake) followers of Jesus. The disciples who obey the Lord's teaching because they know and love their heavenly Father (John 14:23–24). In Matthew 7:21–27, Jesus gave a stern warning to people who hear the words of God but don't act on them:

> *²¹"Not everyone who says to Me, 'Lord, Lord,' shall enter the kingdom of heaven, but he who does the will of My Father in heaven. ²²Many will say to Me in that day, 'Lord, Lord, have we not prophesied in Your name, cast out demons in Your name, and done many wonders in Your name?' ²³And then I will declare to them, 'I never knew you; depart from Me, you who practice lawlessness!"*

Lawlessness, as Acts of Sin; they are deeds that manifest rebellion against God. To be "full of lawlessness" (Matthew 23:28), is to lead a life characterized by wrongdoing.

> *²⁴"Therefore, whoever hears these sayings of Mine, and does them, I will liken him to a wise man who built his house on the rock: ²⁵and the rain descended, the floods came, and the winds blew and beat on that house; and it did not fall, for it was founded on the rock. ²⁶"But everyone who hears these sayings of Mine, and does not do them, will be like a foolish man who built his house on the sand: ²⁷and the rain descended, the floods came, and the winds blew and beat on that house; and it fell. And great was its fall."*

We may fool other people (1 Samuel 16:7), and we may even fool ourselves (Jeremiah 17:9), but we cannot fool God (Psalm 44:21). We should be encouraging Christians and others to seek God's will through obedience. The most powerful tool we have in this task is the Word of God (Hebrews 4:12). Sometimes it can seem words are nothing more than just that - just words. But words can have more weight depending on who's speaking to us. The words a friend or family member says to us will bear more gravity or significance than of an acquaintance. In the same way, because our relationship with God is of highest importance to us, as followers of Christ, we must take into greater consideration His words spoken to us.

The primary way that God speaks to us, is through the Bible (His Word). Bible reading is one of the most important spiritual disciplines that we must grow in, and to miss out on IT, could prove to be more dangerous for us than convenient. Sin begins in the heart, and that's where God looks (1 Samuel 16:7; Jeremiah 17:10; Romans 8:27). If we are not reading the Bible because we are not interested in what God has said, we are guilty of apathy (laziness or unconcerned).

If we are not reading the Bible because we think we don't need to, we are guilty of pride. If we are not reading the Bible because we cannot find the time or we don't consider it important, we are guilty of having wrong priorities. Ouch! We are guilty of having wrong priorities:

> When our priorities are wrong, it means we are seeking the wrong things. When we seek the wrong things, we are only left empty and unsatisfied, longing for more, bigger, and better. Instead, we are to seek after God and make sure the work we are doing is for Him rather than for ourselves.

Jesus said, "Seek first the kingdom of God and his righteousness" (Matthew 6:33, ESV). Jesus also SAID, "To whom much is given, much is required" (Luke 12:48). God expects us to invest our time, resources, passions, and service in that which has eternal value. Those who have God's Word at their fingertips will answer to Him for what they did with that high privilege.

I read in a Pastor Resources "Helping Ministers Grow Healthy Churches" News Letter that: In every generation, we face the danger of longing for the past while fearing the future. And this mix of nostalgia (homesickness or reminiscence) and fear, leads us into a state of complacency; a mission-less faith. We file in and out of the sanctuary week after week, content to recite the same words with our lips, but our hearts remain un-stirred by the truths we confess, and we are less likely to invite others to believe the good news (the gospel).

Please absorb this very carefully; there is no room for complacency in our spiritual walk. We are not to be complacent in studying the Word of God, obeying Him, worshipping Him, praying, fasting, evangelizing, and giving. Don't be complacent in doing all that God expects of you. I often encouraged family, friends, relatives, associates, and many others in churches, and communities world-wide to:

"Be doers of the Word and not hearers only deceiving yourselves."
(James 1:22)

To be a doer of the Word of God means to do more, take action, and be proactive (be active). We do this out of gratitude for what Christ has done for us. We shine our good deeds to proclaim the Lord's glory, not to gain His favor. We prove by the way we live that we have repented of our sins, and turned to God (Matthew 3:8). Taking action and being a doer of the Word can make people take notice because we are living differently from the average person. Some of the most important things we can do are helping to lighten, the burdens of others, freeing people who feel trapped by something, easing oppression, removing chains that bind people, sharing food with the hungry (physical and soul food), and giving people in need a warm place to stay or warm clothing (Isaiah 58:6-7).

In conclusion, do All things with love! Maintain a soft, tenderhearted, heart by seeking to love God above everything else. Then go forward to love and care for your neighbors. Your neighbors are everyone else other than you. First Peter 4:8 (NIV), reads, " Above all, love each other deeply, because love covers over a multitude of sins."

Be a doer of the Word, with much love in your heart. For even the Son of Man (Jesus Christ) came not to be served but to serve others and to give his life as a ransom for many (Matthew 20:28). We Must be doers of the Word! The blessing, is in the doing!

James 4:14, reminds us that *"we don't know what tomorrow will bring and that we're a mist that appears for a short time and then vanishes."* I love, keeping it real! Usually, you can figure out someone's priorities by their appearance, actions, and how they spend their time. When people's priorities are wrong, it does not matter how hard you work. It's like rowing a boat against the current. You put in all the effort and work but don't see a return for your labor. When our priorities are wrong, we are pursuing the wrong things. We're left unsatisfied and empty by seeking the wrong things, longing for something bigger and better. Instead, we should seek God and make sure that our work is for God, not ourselves. I cannot emphasize enough; put God first! Make God, your top priority!

Please pray this prayer:

Eternal God in Heaven; I thank you! I give you all glory, honor, and praise! Father God, help me; help me to make sure, that I am a hearer, and doer of your Word. Help me not to be complacent in my spiritual walk with You, and every area of my life. Father God, I shall be fervent in the Spirit, not lukewarm. Father God, I ask that You deliver all those who are complacent and confused. Help those who are only hearers of your Word, and help those who are casualties of complacency to recover. In the mighty name of Jesus, Amen.

NOTES:

Chapter 12

ALWAYS BE READY, TO GIVE A DEFENSE!

When people ask you, "why do you follow Jesus?" What do you say to them? Well, the apostle Peter said we should always be ready to give reasons, for believing as we do. So, you can tell those who ask you, "why do you follow Jesus?

The main reason I follow Jesus is because He is, the Lord! A person who says, "Jesus is Lord," with a full understanding of what that really means has been divinely enlightened:

1) Jesus is God and has supreme authority over all things.
2) "No one can say, 'Jesus is Lord,' except by the Holy Spirit" (1 Corinthians 12:3).
3) Faith in the Lord Jesus is required for salvation (Acts 16:31).
4) Jesus is Lord; it's the truth, whether or not people acknowledge the fact.
5) Jesus is more than the Messiah:
    - He's more than the Savior!
    - He's the Lord of all!

Someday, all will submit to that truth; God exalted Jesus to the highest place and gave Him the name that is above every name, that at the name of

Jesus every knee should bow, in heaven and on earth and under the earth, and every tongue acknowledge that Jesus Christ is Lord, to the glory of God the Father" (Philippians 2:9–11).

You can also tell those who ask you, "why you follow Jesus, some more reasons:

1) Because Jesus said, 'I have come that you might have life, and have it more abundantly.'
2) Jesus will give you an abundant life!
3) Not only that, He will give you peace with God.
4) Jesus will give you; new purpose and meaning.
5) He will help you overcome the temptations that would destroy your life.

Being a Christian, is the greatest life in this world and following Jesus is the best decision one can ever make. Yes, I realize, choosing Jesus is not something that we automatically do. It's not something that comes naturally to us, so to speak. That's why choosing Jesus is a really big deal to God, it means we finally realize that we cannot do all this on our own. Even though we choose Jesus, it can be easy to get side-tracked when the demands or pressures of life, come knocking at our door. Unfortunately, it is during difficulties when most, lose sight of God. When we get to that point; we must step-back and seek our own personal spiritual revival.

It's amazing what praising God can do in the midst of the most difficult circumstances.

> First Peter 3:14-15, says: *"[14]But even if you should suffer for righteousness' sake, you are blessed. "And do not be afraid of their threats, nor be troubled."*
>
> *[15]But [a]sanctify [b]the Lord God in your hearts, and always be ready to give a defense to everyone who asks you a reason for the hope that is in you, with meekness and fear."*

Following Jesus can give us increased or added trials and persecutions! The apostle Peter is telling us that instead of retaliating against evil; a Christian must focus on sanctifying God in his or her heart. First Peter, Chapter 3, also instructs wives how to behave towards their husbands, and husbands how to behave towards their wives, and exhorts to various things common to all Christians, and particularly to suffer patiently for righteousness's sake.

But why choose Jesus? This is a question every believer or disciple should be able to answer. To follow Jesus, means our lives will be totally different from those around us. One major thing that distinguishes true followers of Jesus from those who just carry the name; is the lifestyle. A lifestyle of obedience to Christ. Sometimes we can carry the name of Christ but not follow Him. I realize that may seem like a harsh thing to speak or say, but seriously; we should all check if we truly follow the Lord Jesus Christ.

Why is that? Well, Because the Lord Jesus Christ Himself gave us a very stern warning, in Matthew 7:21-23:

> *"Not everyone who says to Me, 'Lord, Lord,' shall enter the kingdom of heaven, but he who does the will of My Father in heaven. Many will say to Me in that day, 'Lord, Lord, have we not prophesied in Your name, cast out demons in Your name, and done many wonders in Your name?' And then I will declare to them, 'I never knew you; depart from Me, you who practice lawlessness!'"*

Again, keeping it real! Just think about it! If no one is asking, why you live the way you do; you are probably not modeling Christ well. Don't be deceived or misled; true believers should be different from the world? Is your life different from the world? If not, please remember, God delivered you from worldliness so you could know him and live for him. True Believers; you must live differently than the world because God commands it, and also because the world is in rebellion against God. The world is "separated," or "alienated," from "the life of God" (Ephesians 4:18).

Believers must live differently than the world because God commands it, and also because the world is in rebellion against God. We don't live like the world. The apostle Peter instructs Christians not to fear those who cause them to suffer "for the sake of Christ. So, how believers should choose to respond? Instead of retaliating, always be ready to give a defense to everyone who asks you a reason for the hope that is in you, with meekness and fear.

We as believers, also sanctify the Lord God in our hearts; to sanctify the Lord God in our hearts we must make the Lord, the focus of our thoughts. We internalize God's Word so that we live by every word of it. Sanctifying the Lord God in our hearts means giving our wholehearted allegiance to Jesus Christ and worshiping Him only; despite the cost. Sanctifying the Lord in our hearts simply means to live for Him, not against Him.

When you set-apart or separate Christ as Lord, it will change you. The apostle Peter says, those who observe or watch us, will notice the difference. That difference is hope. Even in the midst of our suffering, our hopefulness should be noticeable. So, Peter instructs us to be ready to answer the question our life should inspire. How can you be so hopeful in such difficult circumstances? Peter expects or anticipates people will become curious or interested. Hopefulness and joy are totally different from the normal human response to suffering. Different So much, that people will be eager or excited to understand it.

So, what will we say when they ask? We must be prepared to give our defense, to make the case for faith in Christ. We need to reject the cultural pressure to keep our beliefs to ourselves. Instead, believers should openly share the good news of redemption through faith in Christ. It matters how we represent or make that case for Christ. We must present it with gentleness and respect. Christians are not called on to condemn those who are curious about our hopefulness. Nor are we to be vindictive, vengeful, or insulting to those who, disagree. Rather, we should explain our faith without harshness or dismissiveness.

In conclusion, following Jesus means striving to be like Him. Jesus always obeyed His Father, so that's what we strive to do (John 8:29; 15:10). To truly follow Christ means to make Him in charge of you and your life. That's what it means to make Jesus Lord of our lives (Romans 10:9; 1 Corinthians 12:3; 2 Corinthians 4:5). Every decision and dream are filtered through His Word with the goal of glorifying Him in everything (1 Corinthians 10:31).

We are not saved by the things we do for Christ (Ephesians 2:8–9) but by what He has done for us. Because of His grace, we want to please Him in everything. All this is accomplished as we allow the Holy Spirit to have complete control of every area of our lives (Ephesians 5:18). He explains the Scriptures (1 Corinthians 2:14), empowers us with spiritual gifts (1 Corinthians 12:4-11), comforts us (John 14:16), and guides us (John 14:26). To follow Christ means we apply the truths we learn from His Word and live as if Jesus walked beside us in person.

NOTES:

www.ingramcontent.com/pod-product-compliance
Lightning Source LLC
LaVergne TN
LVHW091536070526
838199LV00001B/86